D0013407

Contents

Introduction

The disciples endured a frightening storm.

It was a terrifying storm. The apostles thought the ship would founder and they'd all drown. But through the storm, they saw their Savior, walking toward them, reassuring them, calming both their fears and the ferocious winds. Scripture tells us that, after the storm, they "worshiped Jesus and said, 'Truly you are the Son of God!' " (Matt. 14:33)

You encounter storms—you face difficult people, painful situations, hardships, disappointments. When you do, remember the One who's stepping toward you to calm your fears.

Perhaps, when your life storms come, you'll see the Savior more clearly, too.

—Max Lucado

Jesus Can Relate

If you've ever had a day in which you've been blitzkrieged by demands, if you've ever ridden the roller coaster of sorrow and celebration, if you've ever wondered if God in heaven can relate to you on earth...

Take heart. Jesus knows how you feel.

—Max Lucado

1. What kinds of pressures make your days the most pressure filled?

put things off at home.

A Moment With Max

Max shares these insights with us in his book *Eye of the Storm*.

Ponder the following and think about it the next time your world goes from calm to chaos:

Jesus knows how you feel.

His pulse has raced. His eyes have grown weary. His heart has grown heavy. He has had to climb out of bed with a sore throat. He has been kept awake late and has gotten up early. He knows how you feel.

You may have trouble believing that. You probably believe that Jesus knows what it means to endure heavy-duty tragedies. You are no doubt convinced that Jesus is acquainted with sorrow and has wrestled with fear. Most people accept that. But can God relate to the hassles and headaches of my life? Of your life?

For some reason this is harder to believe.

Every page of the Gospels hammers home this crucial principle: God knows how you feel. From the funeral to the factory to the frustration of a demanding schedule. Jesus understands. When you tell God that you've reached your limit, he knows what you mean. When you shake your head at impossible deadlines, he shakes his too. When your plans are interrupted by people who have other plans, he nods in empathy. He has been there. He knows how you feel.

2. How does Max's perspective match your perception of Jesus?

Semalar

3. Describe the difference between the stress of "heavy-duty tragedies" and the stress of everyday living.

A Message from the Word

[1]We have around us many people whose lives tell us what faith means. So let us run the race that is before us and never give up. We should remove from our lives anything that would get in the way and the sin that so easily holds us back. [2]Let us look only to Jesus, the One who began our faith and who makes it perfect. He suffered death on the cross. But he accepted the shame as if it were nothing because of the joy that God put before him. And now he is sitting at the right side of God's throne. [3]Think about Jesus' example. He held on while wicked people were doing evil things to him. So do not get tired and stop trying.

[4]You are struggling against sin, but your struggles have not yet caused you to be killed.

Hebrews 12:1-4

4. How does keeping our eyes on Jesus help us meet the daily struggles of life?

not alone - this isn't all.

5. In what ways do the trivialities of life hinder us in our journey?

Spend too much time on them

6. Some difficulties are consequences of sin, and some are just normal recurrences of life. How do they differ?

More from the Word

4 [14]Since we have a great high priest, Jesus the Son of God, who has gone into
heaven, let us hold on to the faith we have. [15]For our high priest is able to
understand our weaknesses. When he lived on earth, he was tempted in
every way that we are, but he did not sin. [16]Let us, then, feel very sure that
we can come before God's throne where there is grace. There we can
receive mercy and grace to help us when we need it.

Hebrews 4:14-16

7. In what ways does Jesus function in our lives as a priest?

8. What does it mean to you that Jesus has gone through the same kind of bad days that you go through?

9. Knowing that Jesus can relate enables us to approach grace differently in what way?

My Reflections

The Healer knows our hurts, he voluntarily became one of us. He placed himself in our position. He suffered our pains and felt our fears.

Rejection? He felt it. Temptation? He knew it. Loneliness? He experienced it. Death? He tasted it.

And stress? He could write a best-selling book about it.

Why did he do it? One reason. So that when you hurt, you will go to him—your Father and your Physician—and let him heal.

—Max

Journal

What part of my life have I always thought Jesus wouldn't understand?

For Further Study

To study more about Christ's compassion read Matthew 9:35–38; 15:32; Mark 1:40–41; Romans 15:7; Ephesians 4:32; Philippians 2:1–8.

Additional Questions

10. If Jesus were here today, what situations do you think he would find most stressful?

Christian indifference - too worldly

11. What are your most stressful circumstances?

12. What does God's willingness to become human say to you about his compassion for you?

amazing!

Additional Thoughts

Are People Worth It?

What did Jesus know that allowed him to do what he did? What internal code kept his calm from erupting into chaos? He knew the value of people.

—Max Lucado

1. Without giving a name, describe one of the most difficult people you've ever had to deal with.

my daughter-in-law

A Moment With Max

Max shares these insights with us in his book *Eye of the Storm*.

In our house we call 5:00 P.M. the piranha hour. That's the time of day when everyone wants a piece of Mom.

Piranha hours: Parents have them, bosses endure them, secretaries dread them, teachers are besieged by them, and Jesus taught us how to live through them successfully.

When hands extended and voices demanded, Jesus responded with love. He did so because the code within him disarmed the alarm. The code is worth noting: "People are precious."

Review what our Lord faced...

Immense crowds—a Niagara of people followed him everywhere.

Insensitive interruptions—he sought rest and got people.

Incredible demands—crowds of thousands clamored for his touch.

Inept assistance—the one and only time he asked for help, he got a dozen "You're pulling my leg" expressions.

But the calm within Christ never erupted. The alarm never sounded. What did Jesus know that enabled him to do what he did? He knew the incredible value of people. As a result:

He didn't stamp his feet and demand his own way.

He didn't tell the disciples to find another beach where there were no people.

He didn't ask the crowds why they hadn't brought their own food.

He didn't send the apostles back into the field for more training.

Most important, he stayed calm in the midst of chaos. He even paused, in the midst of it all, to pray a prayer of thanks.

2. What is the natural human response to our piranha hours?

Stress out

3. Why do we tend to devalue people when they irritate us?

It interferes with wants + needs plans

A Message from the Word

[38]"You have heard that it was said, 'An eye for an eye, and a tooth for a
tooth.' [39]But I tell you, don't stand up against an evil person. If someone
slaps you on the right cheek, turn to him the other cheek also. [40]If someone
wants to sue you in court and take your shirt, let him have your coat also.
[41]If someone forces you to go with him one mile, go with him two miles.
[42]If a person asks you for something, give it to him. Don't refuse to give to
someone who wants to borrow from you.
[43]"You have heard that it was said, 'Love your neighbor and hate your ene-
mies.' [44]But I say to you, love your enemies. Pray for those who hurt you. [45]If
you do this, you will be true children of your Father in heaven. He causes the
sun to rise on good people and on evil people, and he sends rain to those
who do right and to those who do wrong. [46]If you love only the people who
love you, you will get no reward. Even the tax collectors do that. [47]And if you
are nice only to your friends, you are no better than other people. Even those
who don't know God are nice to their friends. [48]So you must be perfect, just
as your Father in heaven is perfect."

Matthew 5:38-48

4. Describe the crux of the difficulty of loving the unlovable.

Hard on your self - you have to put your (wants & needs) self aside. its hard on your heart & mind" takes alot of time

5. How can Jesus' example help us have patience with the people who aggravate us?

" must love as he loved - the value of each life - very important to Jesus!

6. Explain the temptation to still live by the creed, "an eye for an eye."

"to get even" I didn't deserve that'

More from the Word

14 I praise you because you made me in an amazing and wonderful way.
What you have done is wonderful.
I know this very well.

15 You saw my bones being formed
as I took shape in my mother's body.
When I was put together there,
16 you saw my body as it was formed.
All the days planned for me
were written in your book
before I was one day old.

Psalm 139:14-16

7. How can the way God values people help us to be more patient with others?

Gods love for us' We are not perfect

8. If we are aware that God values us, why do we spend so much energy worrying about daily concerns?

The society we live in interferes with our schedules & time

9. How does the patience we have with ourselves affect the patience we have with others?

same?

My Reflections

When is your piranha hour? When do people in your world demand much and offer little?

What did Jesus know that enabled him to do what he did? He knew how the people felt, and he knew that they were special.

You are precious to him. So precious that he became like you so that you would come to him.

When you struggle, he listens. When you yearn, he responds. When you question, he hears. He has been there.

—Max

Journal

What kind of compassion do I need from God and how can I pass that compassion along?

For Further Study

To study more about the value of people Leviticus 24:17; Jeremiah 31:3; Matthew 6:25-34; Matthew 12:11-12; John 3:16.

Additional Questions

10. How does society place a value on people?

11. How do you think the world would function differently if, for the most part, our society valued humans the way Jesus did?

12. What is the most difficult part of dealing with people?

Additional Thoughts

20

Fishermen Who Don't Fish

The next time the challenges "outside" tempt you to shut the door and stay inside, stay long enough to get warm. Then get out. When those who are called to fish don't fish, they fight.

—Max Lucado

1. Describe the silliest church conflict you've ever heard about.

____

____

____

____

____

____

____

____

A Moment With Max

Max shares these insights with us in his book *Eye of the Storm*.

When those who are called to fish don't fish, they fight.

When energy intended to be used outside is used inside, the result is explosive. Instead of casting nets, we cast stones. Instead of extending helping hands, we point accusing fingers. Instead of being fishers of the lost, we become critics of the saved. Rather than helping the hurting, we hurt the helpers.

The result? Church Scrooges. "Bah humbug" spirituality. Beady eyes searching for warts on others while ignoring the wart on the nose below. Crooked fingers that bypass strengths and point out weaknesses.

Split churches. Poor testimonies. Broken hearts. Legalistic wars.

And, sadly, poor go unfed, confused go uncounseled, and lost go unreached.

When those who are called to fish don't fish, they fight.

But note the other side of this fish tale: When those who are called to fish, fish—they flourish!

Nothing handles a case of gripes like an afternoon service project. Nothing restores perspective better than a visit to a hospital ward. Nothing unites soldiers better than a common task.

Leave soldiers inside the barracks with no time on the front line and see what happens to their attitude. The soldiers will invent things to complain about. Bunks will be too hard. Food will be too cold. Leadership will be too tough. The company will be too stale. Yet place those same soldiers in the trench and let them duck a few bullets, and what was a boring barracks will seem like a haven. The beds will feel great. The food will be almost ideal. The leadership will be courageous. The company will be exciting.

When those who are called to fish, fish—they flourish.

2. How have you seen this principle played out: That we tend to be negative when we have nothing better to do?

____

____

____

____

____

3. Describe what we have been called to do as the body of Christ.

Rom. 13:8

14:12, 13, 19

15-5-7

1 Cor 11-33

12-27

A Message from the Word

[6]Brothers and sisters, by the authority of our Lord Jesus Christ we com-
mand you to stay away from any believer who refuses to work and does not
follow the teaching we gave you. [7]You yourselves know that you should live
as we live. We were not lazy when we were with you. [8]And when we ate
another person's food, we always paid for it. We worked very hard night
and day so we would not be an expense to any of you. [9]We had the right to
ask you to help us, but we worked to take care of ourselves so we would
be an example for you to follow. [10]When we were with you, we gave you
this rule: "Anyone who refuses to work should not eat."
[11]We hear that some people in your group refuse to work. They do nothing
but busy themselves in other people's lives. [12]We command those people
and beg them in the Lord Jesus Christ to work quietly and earn their own
food. [13]But you, brothers and sisters, never become tired of doing good.

2 Thessalonians 3:6-13

4. List some dangers of having too much time on your hands?

5. What is the balance between being too idle and being too driven, in light of our service to God.

____

____

____

____

6. From your experience what are the top three reasons for church conflicts?

____

____

____

____

More from the Word

[11]And Christ gave gifts to people—he made some to be apostles, some to be
prophets, some to go and tell the Good News, and some to have the work of
caring for and teaching God's people. [12]Christ gave those gifts to prepare God's
holy people for the work of serving, to make the body of Christ stronger. [13]This
work must continue until we are all joined together in the same faith and in
the same knowledge of the Son of God. We must become like a mature person,
growing until we become like Christ and have his perfection.
[14]Then we will no longer be babies. We will not be tossed about like a
ship that the waves carry one way and then another. We will not be influ-
enced by every new teaching we hear from people who are trying to fool
us. They make plans and try any kind of trick to fool people into following
the wrong path. [15]No! Speaking the truth with love, we will grow up in
every way into Christ, who is the head. [16]The whole body depends on
Christ, and all the parts of the body are joined and held together. Each part
does its own work to make the whole body grow and be strong with love.

Ephesians 4:11-16

7. What do you consider to be the mission of the church?

8. What does the idleness of the church say about our understanding of our mission?

9. If the church is like a body, how are church conflicts like cancer?

My Reflections

Once [Jesus] felt their hurts, he couldn't help but heal their hurts. He was moved in the stomach by their needs. He was so touched by their needs that he forgot his own needs. He was so moved by the people's hurts that he put his hurts on the back burner.

Maybe that's why God brings hurting people into your world, too. All solitude and no service equals selfishness. Some solitude and some service, however, equals perspective.

—Max

Journal

How balanced is my perspective in terms of helping myself and helping others?

Next

For Further Study

To study more about the role of the church read Acts 12:5; 15:36–16:5; Romans 12:4–16; 1 Corinthians 10:31–33; 12:27–30; 14:26–28; Hebrews 10:24–25; James 4:11; 1 Peter 3:8-9.

Additional Questions

10. Give some examples of churches or people you have seen with too much time on their hands.

11. What escalates disagreements in the church to the point of anger?

12. Why do we often feel more passionately about issues having to do with church than other issues?

Additional Thoughts

A Shattered View of God

There is a window in your heart through which you can see God. Once upon a time that window was clear. Your view of God was crisp. You could see God as vividly as you could see a gentle valley or hillside. The glass was clear, the pane unbroken.

Then, suddenly, the window cracked. A pebble broke the window. A pebble of pain.

—Max Lucado

1. What kinds of circumstances cause such pain in our lives that our perception of God is altered?

____

____

____

____

____

____

A Moment With Max

Max shares these insights with us in his book *Eye of the Storm*.

Perhaps the stone struck when you were a child and a parent left home—forever. Maybe the rock hit in adolescence when your heart was broken. Maybe you made it into adulthood before the window was cracked. But then the pebble came.

Whatever the pebble's form, the result was the same—a shattered window. The pebble missiled into the pane and shattered it. The crash echoed down the halls of your heart...and suddenly God was not so easy to see. The view that had been so crisp had changed. You turned to see God, and his figure was distorted. It was hard to see him through the pain. It was hard to see him through the fragments of hurt.

You were puzzled. God wouldn't allow something like this to happen, would he? Tragedy and travesty weren't on the agenda of the One you had seen, were they? Had you been fooled? Had you been blind?

The moment the pebble struck, the glass became a reference point for you. From then on, there was life before the pain and life after the pain. Before your pain, the view was clear; God seemed so near. After your pain, well, he was harder to see. He seemed a bit distant . . . harder to perceive. Your pain distorted the view—not eclipsed it, but distorted it.

2. Why do painful circumstances sometimes make us doubt God's good intentions toward us?

3. Describe the path that you think is necessary to fix a pain-distorted view of God.

A Message from the Word

1I cry out to God;
I call to God, and he will hear me.
2I look for the Lord on the day of trouble.
All night long I reach out my hands,
but I cannot be comforted.
3When I remember God, I become upset;
when I think, I become afraid.
4You keep my eyes from closing.
I am too upset to say anything.
5I keep thinking about the old days,
the years of long ago.
6At night I remember my songs.
I think and I ask myself:
7"Will the Lord reject us forever?
Will he never be kind to us again?
8Is his love gone forever?
Has he stopped speaking for all time?
9Has God forgotten mercy?
Is he too angry to pity us?"

Psalm 77:1-9

4. Add some questions to this Psalmist's question that reflect our musings when we face great pain.

___

___

___

5. What are some reasons we assume life should be pain-free?

___

___

___

6. What are the emotions we feel when we face great pain in life?

More from the Word

[22]Immediately Jesus told his followers to get into the boat and go ahead of

him across the lake. He stayed there to send the people home. [23]After he
had sent them away, he went by himself up into the hills to pray. It was late,
and Jesus was there alone. [24]By this time, the boat was already far away from
land. It was being hit by waves, because the wind was blowing against it.
[25]Between three and six o'clock in the morning, Jesus came to them,
walking on the water. [26]When his followers saw him walking on the water,
they were afraid. They said, "It's a ghost!" and cried out in fear.
[27]But Jesus quickly spoke to them, "Have courage! It is I. Do not be afraid."

Matthew 14:22-27

7. How does the storm the disciples experienced compare to storms of pain in our lives?

8. How do you recognize Jesus presence in the storms you encounter?

9. Why do we sometimes not recognize God when he comes to us in the midst of our pain, just as these disciples didn't recognize Jesus in the storm?

My Reflections

Jesus came. He finally came. But between verse 24—being buffeted by waves, and verse 25—when Jesus appeared, a thousand questions are asked.

Questions you have probably asked, too. Perhaps you know the angst of being suspended between verse 24 and 25. Maybe you're riding a storm, searching the coastline for a light, a glimmer of hope. You know that Jesus knows what you are going through. You know that he's aware of your storm. But as hard as you look to find him, you can't see him.

—Max

Journal

What kind of painful storm am I riding through right now?

For Further Study

To study more about dealing with pain read Eccl. 2:21–25; Psalm 6:1–7; 31:9–13; 34:17–22; 62:5–8 Revelation 21:1–4.

Additional Questions

10. What else would you compare pain to besides a storm?

11. How do you get perspective when you wonder, "Is God doing this to me, or is this just life happening?"

12. How long do you think it takes to restore a pain-distorted view of God?

Additional Thoughts

A Far Off Destination

Remember this: God may not do what you want, but he will do what is right and best. He's the Father of forward motion. Trust him. He will get you home. And the trials of the trip will be lost in the joys of the feast.

—Max Lucado

1. Describe the worst trip you've ever endured.

A Moment With Max

Max shares these insights with us in his book *Eye of the Storm*.

For me, six hours on the road is a small price to pay for my mom's strawberry cake. I don't mind the drive because I know the reward. I have three decades of Thanksgivings under my belt, literally. As I drive, I can taste the turkey, hear the dinner-table laughter, and smell the smoke from the fireplace.

I can endure the journey because I know the destiny.

My daughters have forgotten the destiny. After all, they are young. Children easily forget. Besides, the road is strange, and the dark night has come. They can't see where we're going. It's my job, as their father, to guide them.

I try to help them see what they can't see.

Perhaps that's how the apostle Paul stayed motivated. He had a clear vision of the reward.

"Therefore we do not lose heart. Though outwardly we are wasting away, yet inwardly we are being renewed day by day…So we fix our eyes not on what is seen, but on what is unseen."

It's not easy to get three girls under the age of seven to see a city they can't see. But it's necessary.

It's not easy to us to see a City we've never seen, either, especially when the road is bumpy, the hour is late, and companions are wanting to cancel the trip and take up residence in a motel. It's not easy to fix your eyes on what is unseen. But it's necessary.

2. What do you consider to be the greatest challenge to delayed gratification?

3. List some elements of the Christian walk that require an acceptance of delayed gratification.

A Message from the Word

16So we do not give up. Our physical body is becoming older and weaker,
but our spirit inside us is made new every day. 17We have small troubles for
a while now, but they are helping us gain an eternal glory that is much
greater than the troubles. 18We set our eyes not on what we see but on
what we cannot see. What we see will last only a short time, but what we
cannot see will last forever.

1We know that our body—the tent we live in here on earth—will be
destroyed. But when that happens, God will have a house for us. It will not
be a house made by human hands; instead, it will be a home in heaven that
will last forever. 2But now we groan in this tent. We want God to give us our
heavenly home, 3because it will clothe us so we will not be naked. 4While
we live in this body, we have burdens, and we groan. We do not want to be
naked, but we want to be clothed with our heavenly home. Then this body
that dies will be fully covered with life. 5This is what God made us for, and
he has given us the Spirit to be a guarantee for this new life.

2 Corinthians 4:16—5:5

4. In what ways do we battle between the seen and the unseen in our day to day lives?

5. For you, what are the things about heaven will make it worth enduring the troubles of this life?

6. What role does faith play in this struggle of keeping our sights on the unseen?

More from the Word

35So do not lose the courage you had in the past, which has a great reward.
36You must hold on, so you can do what God wants and receive what he
has promised. 37For in a very short time,

"The One who is coming will come
and will not be delayed.
38The person who is right with me
will live by trusting in me.
But if he turns back with fear,
I will not be pleased with him."

39But we are not those who turn back and are lost. We are people who
have faith and are saved.

1Faith means being sure of the things we hope for and knowing that something is real even if we do not see it.

Hebrews 10:35—11:1

7. What can we put our confidence in when perservering is at its most difficult?

8. Describe someone who lives by faith.

9. Of all the kinds of journeys you can think of, (road trips, camping, hiking, railroad, stagecoach, etc) how would you best describe your life's journey?

My Reflections

For some of you, the journey has been long. Very long and stormy. In no way do I wish to minimize the difficulties that you have had to face along the way. Some of you have shouldered burdens that few of us could ever carry. You have bid farewell to life-long partners. You have been robbed of life-long dreams. You have been given bodies that can't sustain your spirit. You have spouses who can't tolerate your faith. You have bills that outnumber the paychecks and challenges that outweigh the strength.

And you are tired.

Let me encourage you...It's worth it.

—Max

Journal

If I compare my life to a trip or vacation, what part of the trip am I in right now?

For Further Study

To study more about endurance read Romans 5:1-5; 15:4-5; 1 Tim 6:11; 2 Tim 2:3-13; Hebrews 12:2-7; James 1:2-4; James 1:12.

Additional Questions

10. What do you think is the greatest challenge of persevering through hard times?

11. How can you best stay focused on the rewards at the end of the journey?

12. In what ways does prayer help you to persevere?

Additional Thoughts

Lesson 6

Storms of Doubt

"If God is so good, why do I sometimes feel so bad?"

"If his message is so clear, why do I get so confused?"

"If the Father is in control, why do good people have gut-wrenching problems?"

—Max Lucado

1. What are some other tough questions that we face when we're are dealing with doubt?

A Moment With Max

Max shares these insights with us in his book *Eye of the Storm*.

Their question—What hope do we have of surviving a stormy night?

My question—Where is God when his world is stormy?

Doubtstorms: turbulent days when the enemy is too big, the task too great, the future too bleak, and the answers too few.

Every so often a storm will come and I'll look up into the blackening sky and say, "God, a little light, please?"

The light came for the disciples. A figure came to them walking on the water. It wasn't what they expected. Perhaps they were looking for angels to descend or heaven to open. Maybe they were listening for a divine proclamation to still the storm. We don't know what they were looking for. But one thing is for sure, they weren't looking for Jesus to come walking on the water....and since Jesus came in a way they didn't expect, they almost missed seeing the answer to their prayers.

And unless we look, and listen closely, we risk making the same mistake. God's lights in our dark nights are as numerous as the stars, if only we'll look for them.

2. Describe a time when God has come to you or someone you know in a time of darkness.

3. On what do we base our expectations of how God will help us?

A Message from the Word

25Between three and six o'clock in the morning, Jesus came to them, walk-
ing on the water. 26When his followers saw him walking on the water, they
were afraid. They said, "It's a ghost!" and cried out in fear.
27But Jesus quickly spoke to them, "Have courage! It is I. Do not be afraid."
28Peter said, "Lord, if it is really you, then command me to come to you on
the water."
29Jesus said, "Come."
And Peter left the boat and walked on the water to Jesus. 30But when
Peter saw the wind and the waves, he became afraid and began to sink. He
shouted, "Lord, save me!"
31Immediately Jesus reached out his hand and caught Peter. Jesus said,
"Your faith is small. Why did you doubt?"
32After they got into the boat, the wind became calm. 33Then those who
were in the boat worshiped Jesus and said, "Truly you are the Son of God!"

Matthew 14:25-33

4. What are some theories about why Jesus was unrecognizable to the disciples?

____

____

____

____

5. Why do you think Peter wanted to go to Jesus on the water rather than asking Jesus to come to him?

____

____

____

____

6. How do you think faith enables miracles such as Peter standing on water?

____

____

____

____

____

More from the Word

[22]One day Jesus and his followers got into a boat, and he said to them, "Let's
go across the lake." And so they started across. [23]While they were sailing,
Jesus fell asleep. A very strong wind blew up on the lake, causing the boat
to fill with water, and they were in danger.
[24]The followers went to Jesus and woke him, saying, "Master! Master! We
will drown!"
Jesus got up and gave a command to the wind and the waves. They stopped,
and it became calm. [25]Jesus said to his followers, "Where is your faith?"
The followers were afraid and amazed and said to each other, "Who is this
that commands even the wind and the water, and they obey him?"

Luke 8:22-25

7. After having witnessed Jesus' power and miracles, why do you think the disciples were still amazed when he worked a miracle?

____

____

____

____

____

8. Give some possible reasons why Jesus would have been sleeping during a storm.

9. Do you think the disciple's lack of faith centered on their fear of the storm, or their inability to calm the storm?

My Reflections

"When Jesus comes," the disciples in the boat may have thought, "he'll split the sky. The sea will be calm. The clouds will disperse."

"When God comes," we doubters think, "all pain will flee. Life will be tranquil. No questions will remain."

And because we look for the bonfire, we miss the candle. Because we listen for the shout, we miss the whisper.

But it is in burnished candles that God comes, and through whispered promises he speaks: "When you doubt, look around; I am closer than you think."

—Max

Journal

What are my expectations of how God will meet me in my life?

For Further Study

To study more about doubts read Matthew 13:57–58; Mark 16:14–18; James 1:5–7; Jude 1:22–23.

Additional Questions

10. What kinds of things make us doubt God?

11. How different do you think our eyes would be if we chose faith more often than fear?

12. Why is God so insulted by disbelief?

Additional Thoughts

Facing Impossible Odds

*Jesus did not try to do it by himself.
Why should you?*

—Max Lucado

1. Describe a time when you or someone you know needed a miracle.

____

____

____

____

____

____

____

____

____

A Moment With Max

Max shares these insights with us in his book *Eye of the Storm*.

"He went up on a mountainside by Himself to pray."

Jesus faced an impossible task. More than five thousand people were ready to fight a battle he had not come to fight. How could he show them that he didn't come to be a king, but to be a sacrifice? How could he take their eyes off an earthly kingdom so that they would see the spiritual one? How could they see the eternal when they only had eyes for the temporal?

What Jesus dreamed of doing and what he seemed about to do were separated by an impossible gulf. So Jesus prayed.

He prayed for the impossible to happen.

Maybe he didn't ask for anything. Maybe he just stood quietly in the presence of the Presence and basked in the Majesty.

Maybe he lifted his head out of the confusion of earth long enough to hear the solution of heaven. Perhaps he was reminded that hard hearts don't faze the Father. That problem people don't perturb the Eternal One.

We don't know what he did or what he said. But we do know the result. The hill became a steppingstone; the storm became a path, and the disciples saw Jesus as they had never seen him before.

During the storm, Jesus prayed. The sky darkened. The winds howled. Yet he prayed. The people grumbled. The disciples doubted. Yet he prayed. When forced to choose between the muscles of men and the mountain of prayer, he prayed.

2. What keeps us from choosing prayer when we face the impossible?

____

____

____

____

3. Why do you think prayer seems like such a passive activity at times?

____

____

____

____

A Message from the Word

17 A man answered, "Teacher, I brought my son to you. He has an evil spirit in
him that stops him from talking. 18 When the spirit attacks him, it throws him
on the ground. Then my son foams at the mouth, grinds his teeth, and becomes
very stiff. I asked your followers to force the evil spirit out, but they couldn't."
19 Jesus answered, "You people have no faith. How long must I stay with
you? How long must I put up with you? Bring the boy to me."
20 So the followers brought him to Jesus. As soon as the evil spirit saw
Jesus, it made the boy lose control of himself, and he fell down and rolled
on the ground, foaming at the mouth.
21 Jesus asked the boy's father, "How long has this been happening?"
The father answered, "Since he was very young. 22 The spirit often throws
him into a fire or into water to kill him. If you can do anything for him,
please have pity on us and help us."
23 Jesus said to the father, "You said, 'If you can!' All things are possible for
the one who believes."
24 Immediately the father cried out, "I do believe! Help me to believe more!"
25 When Jesus saw that a crowd was quickly gathering, he ordered the evil
spirit, saying, "You spirit that makes people unable to hear or speak, I command you to come out of this boy and never enter him again!"
26 The evil spirit screamed and caused the boy to fall on the ground again.
Then the spirit came out. The boy looked as if he were dead, and many people said, "He is dead!" 27 But Jesus took hold of the boy's hand and helped
him to stand up.
28 When Jesus went into the house, his followers began asking him privately,
"Why couldn't we force that evil spirit out?"
29 Jesus answered, "That kind of spirit can only be forced out by prayer."

Mark 9:17-29

4. What was the special power of prayer in this impossible situation?

5. In what ways does prayer make such a difference in the impossible situations we face?

____

____

____

____

____

6. How do you think your life would be different if you prayed more frequently and more fervently?

____

____

____

____

____

More from the Word

[13]Anyone who is having troubles should pray. Anyone who is happy should sing praises. [14]Anyone who is sick should call the church's elders. They should pray for and pour oil on the person in the name of the Lord. [15]And the prayer that is said with faith will make the sick person well; the Lord will heal that person. And if the person has sinned, the sins will be forgiven. [16]Confess your sins to each other and pray for each other so God can heal you. When a believing person prays, great things happen. [17]Elijah was a human being just like us. He prayed that it would not rain, and it did not rain on the land for three and a half years! [18]Then Elijah prayed again, and the rain came down from the sky, and the land produced crops again.

James 5:13–18

7. How do you know if a prayer has been effective?

8. In what ways do you think prayer effects healing?

9. If we believe prayer makes a difference, what keeps us from praying?

My Reflections

There are crevasses in your life that you cannot cross alone. There are hearts in your world that you cannot change without help. There are mountains that you cannot climb until you climb His mountain.

Climb it. You will be amazed.

—Max

Journal

What impossible situation do I need to turn over to God in prayer?

For Further Study

To study more about praying through the impossible read Psalm 32:6–7; Psalm 61:1–5; Psalm 66:16–20; Proverbs 15:29; Isaiah 30:15; Matthew 17:20; Mark 10:24–27.

Additional Questions

10. Describe the most amazing answer to prayer you have ever witnessed or heard about.

11. Why do you think prayer is the key to the impossible?

12. What does God gain from our prayers?

Additional Thoughts

Why? Why? Why?

God owes no one anything. No explanations. No excuses. No help. God has no debt, no outstanding balance, no favors to return. God owes no man anything.

Which makes the fact that he gave us everything even more astounding.

—Max Lucado

1. If God owes us nothing, why do we question him when things go wrong?

____

____

____

____

____

____

____

____

A Moment With Max

Max shares these insights with us in his book *Eye of the Storm*.

Talk about calm becoming chaos . . .

The first thing to go is his empire. Stocks go flat and Job goes broke. There he sits in his leather chair and soon-to-be-auctioned-off mahogany desk when the phone rings with news of calamity number two:

The kids were at a resort for the holidays when a storm blew in and took them with it.

Shell-shocked and dumbfounded, Job looks out the window into the sky that seems to be getting darker by the minute. He starts praying, telling God that things can't get any worse, and that's exactly what happens...

Job is in his eyes, a good man. And a good man, he reasons, deserves a good answer.

Yet his question still hasn't been answered: "God, why is this happening to me?"

So God speaks....Questions rush forth. They pour like sheets of rain out of the clouds. They splatter in the chambers of Job's heart with a wildness and a beauty and a terror that leave every Job who has ever lived drenched and speechless, watching the Master redefine who is who in the universe. God's questions aren't intended to teach; they are intended to stun. They aren't intended to enlighten; they are intended to awaken. They aren't intended to stir the mind; they are intended to bend the knees.

Finally Job's feeble hand lifts, and God stops long enough for him to respond. "I am nothing—how could I ever find the answers? I lay my hand upon my mouth in silence. I have said too much already."

God's message has connected.

2. Describe a time in your life when you felt "put in your place" by God.

____

____

____

3. Trace the logic that causes us to blame God when difficult things happen in our lives.

____

____

A Message from the Word

12These people are wicked,
always at ease, and getting richer.
13So why have I kept my heart pure?
Why have I kept my hands from doing wrong?
14I have suffered all day long;
I have been punished every morning.
15God, if I had decided to talk like this,
I would have let your people down.
16I tried to understand all this,
but it was too hard for me to see
17until I went to the Temple of God.
Then I understood what will happen to them.
18You have put them in danger;
you cause them to be destroyed.
19They are destroyed in a moment;
they are swept away by terrors.
20It will be like waking from a dream.
Lord, when you rise up, they will disappear.
21When my heart was sad
and I was angry,
22I was senseless and stupid.
I acted like an animal toward you.
23But I am always with you;
you have held my hand.
24You guide me with your advice,
and later you will receive me in honor.
25I have no one in heaven but you;
I want nothing on earth besides you.
26My body and my mind may become weak,
but God is my strength.
He is mine forever.

Psalm 73:12-26

4. Why, as in this Psalm, does it sometimes seem that evil reaps more rewards than righteousness?

5. In the end, no matter how much we doubt or wonder how do we come back, as this psalmist did, to God's presence as our source of strength and joy?

6. What are the promises that we do have, even when it seems like misfortune always finds us?

More from the Word

35 Can anything separate us from the love Christ has for us? Can troubles or problems or sufferings or hunger or nakedness or danger or violent death?
36 As it is written in the Scriptures:

"For you we are in danger of death all the time.

People think we are worth no more than sheep to be killed."
[37]But in all these things we have full victory through God who showed
his love for us. [38]Yes, I am sure that neither death, nor life, nor angels, nor
ruling spirits, nothing now, nothing in the future, no powers, [39]nothing
above us, nothing below us, nor anything else in the whole world will ever
be able to separate us from the love of God that is in Christ Jesus our Lord.

Romans 8:35-39

7. In what ways, if any, does it alter your view of difficulties to know that God's love is constant through them?

____

____

____

____

8. Why do you think God sometimes seem far away when times are tough?

____

____

____

____

____

9. If God is not going to remove difficulties from our lives, do you think it is enough that he promises to be with us through them?

____

____

____

____

My Reflections

Something tells me that Job would do it all again, if that's what it took to hear God's voice and stand in the Presence. Even if God left him with his bedsores and bills, Job would do it again.

For God gave Job more than Job ever dreamed. God gave Job Himself.

—Max

Journal

I need reassurance of God's presence in these areas...

For Further Study

To study more about trials and difficulties read 2 Corinthians 12:7–10; 2 Timothy 2:1–7; James 1:2–7; 1 Peter 1:3–9.

Additional Questions

10. Name some proverbs, cliches, or contemporary logic that people dole out as advice during difficult times.

11. Do you think, as some people say, that we wouldn't appreciate the good if we didn't have the bad?

12. Describe a time when you were aware of God's presence in a difficult situation.

Additional Thoughts

Fear, Fantasy or Faith?

"They saw Jesus . . . walking on the water; and they were terrified."

—Max Lucado

1. Describe a time when something very unexpected terrified you.

A Moment With Max

Max shares these insights with us in his book *Eye of the Storm*.

Faith is often the child of fear.

Fear propelled Peter out of the boat. He'd ridden these waves before. He knew what these storms could do. He'd heard the stories. He'd seen the wreckage. He knew the widows. He knew the storm could kill. And he wanted out...

Look into his eyes tonight and see fear—a suffocating, heart-racing fear of a man who has no way out.

But out of this fear would be born an act of faith, for faith is often the child of fear.

If Peter had seen Jesus walking on the water during a calm, peaceful day, do you think that he would have walked out to him?

Nor do I.

Had the lake been carpet smooth and the journey pleasant, do you think that Peter would have begged Jesus to take him on a stroll across the top of the water? Doubtful.

But give a man a choice between sure death and a crazy chance, and he'll take the chance . . . every time.

Great acts of faith are seldom born out of calm calculation.

It wasn't logic that caused Moses to raise his staff on the bank of the Red Sea.

It wasn't medical research that convinced Naaman to dip seven times in the river.

It wasn't common sense that caused Paul to abandon the Law and embrace grace.

And it wasn't a confident committee that prayed in a small room in Jerusalem for Peter's release from prison. It was a fearful, desperate, band of backed-into-a-corner believers. It was a church with no options. A congregation of have-nots pleading for help.

And never were they stronger.

At the beginning of every act of faith, there is often a seed of fear.

2. How do you respond to that last statement that "at the beginning of every act of faith there is often a seed of fear"?

____

____

____

____

3. In what ways do you think our desperation fuels our faith?

A Message from the Word

[25]Among them was a woman who had been bleeding for twelve years. [26]She
had suffered very much from many doctors and had spent all the money
she had, but instead of improving, she was getting worse. [27]When the
woman heard about Jesus, she came up behind him in the crowd and
touched his coat. [28]She thought, "If I can just touch his clothes, I will be
healed." [29]Instantly her bleeding stopped, and she felt in her body that she
was healed from her disease.
[30]At once Jesus felt power go out from him. So he turned around in the
crowd and asked, "Who touched my clothes?"
[31]His followers said, "Look at how many people are pushing against you!
And you ask, 'Who touched me?' "
[32]But Jesus continued looking around to see who had touched him. [33]The
woman, knowing that she was healed, came and fell at Jesus' feet. Shaking
with fear, she told him the whole truth. [34]Jesus said to her, "Dear woman, you
are made well because you believed. Go in peace; be healed of your disease."

Mark 5:25-34

4. What parallels can you draw between Peter's jumping out of the boat and this woman touching Jesus in a crowd?

5. What do you think the feelings were like that let her know she had been healed?

6. Describe the ways that fear can both prompt our faith and destroy our faith.

More from the Word

1 The Lord is my light and the one who saves me.
    I fear no one.
The Lord protects my life;
    I am afraid of no one.

4 I ask only one thing from the Lord.
    This is what I want:
Let me live in the Lord's house
    all my life.
Let me see the Lord's beauty
    and look with my own eyes at his Temple.

5 During danger he will keep me safe in his shelter.
He will hide me in his Holy Tent,
or he will keep me safe on a high mountain.

7 Lord, hear me when I call;
have mercy and answer me.
8 My heart said of you, "Go, worship him."
So I come to worship you, Lord.

Psalm 27:1, 4-5, 7-8

7. What kinds of things do you and your peers fear in life?

8. What convinces you, as Peter was convinced, that getting to God is better than sitting in your fear?

9. As you compare your fears to Peter's fear for safety, what would be your equivalent of walking on water (that risk you would take to get to where God is)?

My Reflections

Salvation is God's sudden, calming presence during the stormy seas of our lives. We hear his voice; we take the step.

We, like Peter, are aware of two facts: We are going down and God is standing up. So we scramble out. We leave behind the Titanic of self-righteousness and stand on the solid path of God's grace.

And, surprisingly, we are able to walk on water. Death is disarmed. Failures are forgivable. Life has real purpose. And God is not only within sight, he is within reach.

—Max

Journal

On what issues do I need to take a step out of the boat?

For Further Study

To study more about fear read Psalm 56:3–4; 112:1–9; Matthew 10:23–31; 1 Peter 3:13–17; 1 John 4:18.

Additional Questions

10. What do you think Peter brought out of the storm experience that the other disciples (who stayed in the boat) didn't?

11. What does prayer have to do with our ability to bring God into the midst of our fears?

12. How *do* you think Peter was able to walk on water?

Additional Thoughts

Lesson 10

The Inconvenience of Inadequacy

I'm not one who easily envisions a smiling God. A weeping God, yes. An angry God, OK. A mighty God, you bet. But a chuckling God? It seems too . . . too . . . too unlike what God should do—and be. Which just shows how much I know—or don't know—about God.

—Max Lucado

1. What about people do you think makes God smile?

A Moment With Max

Max shares these insights with us in his book *Eye of the Storm*.

One would think that the Creator would not be easily impressed. But something about this woman brought a sparkle to his eyes and, most likely, a smile to his face.

The woman is desperate. Her daughter is demon possessed.

The Cannaanite woman has no right to ask anything of Jesus. She is not a Jew. She is not a disciple. She offers no money…But that doesn't slow her down. She persists in her plea.

"Have mercy on me!"

Matthew notes that Jesus says nothing at first. Nothing. He doesn't open his mouth. Why?

I think that he was admiring her. I think that it did his heart good to see some spunky faith for a change. I think that it refreshed him to see someone asking him to do the very thing he came to do—give great gifts to unworthy children.

How strange that we don't allow him to do it more often for us.

Perhaps the most amazing response to God's gift is our reluctance to accept it. We want it. But on our terms. For some odd reason, we feel better if we earn it. So we create religious hoops and hop through them—making God a trainer, us his pets, and religion a circus.

The Canaanite woman knew better. She had no resume. She claimed no heritage. She had no earned degrees. She knew only two things: Her daughter was weak and Jesus was strong.

2. Do you think God routinely does what Jesus did here: Give help when it is undeserved just because someone asks? Give examples.

___

___

___

___

3. Why is it sometimes easier to reach out on behalf of someone else who is helpless than for ourselves when we are helpless?

___

___

A Message from the Word

1I cry out to the Lord;
    I pray to the Lord for mercy.
2I pour out my problems to him;
    I tell him my troubles.
3When I am afraid,
    you, Lord, know the way out.
In the path where I walk,
    a trap is hidden for me.
4Look around me and see.
    No one cares about me.
I have no place of safety;
    no one cares if I live.

5Lord, I cry out to you.
    I say, "You are my protection.
        You are all I want in this life."
6Listen to my cry,
    because I am helpless.
Save me from those who are chasing me,
    because they are too strong for me.
7Free me from my prison,
    and then I will praise your name.
Then good people will surround me,
    because you have taken care of me.

Psalm 142:1-7

4. In what ways do we pray differently when we pray out of helplessness?

5. How do you think desperation affects faith?

6. If we aren't approaching God from a position of helplessness, then how are we usually approaching him?

More from the Word

7So that I would not become too proud of the wonderful things that were shown to me, a painful physical problem was given to me. This problem was a messenger from Satan, sent to beat me and keep me from being too proud. 8I begged the Lord three times to take this problem away from me. 9But he said to me, "My grace is enough for you. When you are weak, my power is made perfect in you." So I am very happy to brag about my weaknesses. Then Christ's power can live in me. 10For this reason I am happy when I have weaknesses, insults, hard times, sufferings, and all kinds of troubles for Christ. Because when I am weak, then I am truly strong.

2 Corinthians 12:7–10

7. Describe the process of making peace with your own weaknesses.

8. Describe any experience that you've had similar to Paul's where you prayed for a specific help from God, but it didn't come.

9. Why do you think "helplessness" is a repulsive concept to our culture?

My Reflections

We prefer to get salvation the old-fashioned way: We earn it. To accept grace is to admit failure, a step we are hesitant to take. We opt to impress God with how good we are rather than confessing how great he is. We dizzy

ourselves with doctrine. Burden ourselves with rules. Think that God will smile on our efforts.

He doesn't.

God's smile is not for the healthy hiker who boasts that he made the journey alone. It is instead, for the crippled leper who begs God for a back on which to ride.

—Max

Journal

In what areas do I need to admit my own helplessness?

For Further Study

To study more about our need for God read Psalm 40:17; 109: 22–25; Matthew 9:35–38; Philippians 3:7–11.

Additional Questions

10. How do we typically view helplessness in our culture?

11. How does God's perspective on helplessness, or inadequacy, differ from ours?

12. What are the worst things about feeling inadequate?

Additional Thoughts

Overwhelmed by Gratitude

Worship is when you're aware that what you've been given is far greater than what you can give. Worship is the awareness that were it not for his touch, you'd still be hobbling and hurting bitter and broken. Worship is the half-glazed expression on the parched face of a desert pilgrim as he discovers that the oasis is not a mirage. —*Max Lucado*

1. What does our worship teach us about our understanding of God?

____

____

____

____

____

____

____

A Moment With Max

Max shares these insights with us in his book *Eye of the Storm*.

Matthew, still the great economizer of words, gave us another phrase on which I wish he would have elaborated:

"They praised the God of Israel."

I wonder how they did that? I feel more certain of what they didn't do than of what they did do. I feel confident that they didn't form a praise committee. I feel confident that they didn't make any robes. I feel confident that they didn't sit in rows and stare at the back of each other's heads.

I doubt seriously if they wrote a creed on how they were to praise this God they had never before worshiped. I can't picture them getting into an argument over technicalities. I doubt if they felt it had to be done indoors.

And I know they didn't wait until the Sabbath to do it.

In all probability, they just did it. Each one—in his or her own way, with his or her own heart—just praised Jesus. Perhaps some people came and fell at Jesus' feet. Perhaps some shouted his name. Maybe a few just went up on the hillside, looked into the sky, and smiled.

I can picture a mom and dad standing speechless before the Healer as they hold their newly healed baby.

I can envision a leper staring in awe at the One who took away his terror.

I can imagine throngs of people pushing and shoving. Wanting to get close. Not to request anything or demand anything, but just to say "thank you."

Perhaps some tried to pay Jesus, but what payment would have been sufficient?

Perhaps some tried to return his gift with another, but what could a person give that would express the gratitude?

All the people could do was exactly what Matthew said they did. "They praised the God of Israel."

2. Think of a time when you felt caught up in worship or awe of God. What was it like?

____

____

____

____

____

3. For you, what kinds of circumstance are most conducive to worshiping God?

A Message from the Word

[2]Praise the LORD for the glory of his name;
 worship the LORD because he is holy.
[3]The LORD's voice is heard over the sea.
 The glorious God thunders;
  the LORD thunders over the ocean.
[4]The LORD's voice is powerful;
 the LORD's voice is majestic.
[5]The LORD's voice breaks the trees;
 the LORD breaks the cedars of Lebanon.
[6]He makes the land of Lebanon dance like a calf
 and Mount Hermon jump like a baby bull.
[7]The LORD's voice makes the lightning flash.
[8]The LORD's voice shakes the desert;
 the LORD shakes the Desert of Kadesh.
[9]The LORD's voice shakes the oaks
 and strips the leaves off the trees.
  In his Temple everyone says, "Glory to God!"
[10]The LORD controls the flood.
 The LORD will be King forever.
[11]The LORD gives strength to his people;
 the LORD blesses his people with peace.

Psalm 29:2-11

4. If you could summarize this psalm of worship into one statement about God, what would it be?

___

___

___

___

5. Describe the difference between worshipping God for "who he is" and praising him for "what he's done."

___

___

___

___

6. How does music affect our worship today?

___

___

___

___

More from the Word

1Sing to the LORD a new song;
sing to the LORD, all the earth.
2Sing to the LORD and praise his name;
every day tell how he saves us.
3Tell the nations of his glory;
tell all peoples the miracles he does,

4 because the LORD is great; he should be praised at all times.
He should be honored more than all the gods,
5 because all the gods of the nations are only idols,
but the LORD made the heavens.
6 The LORD has glory and majesty;
he has power and beauty in his Temple.

Psalm 96:1-6

7. What attribute of God most awes you?

8. What work of God most amazes you?

9. What does our worship tell God about our character?

My Reflections

We have tried to make a science out of worship. We can't do that. We can't do that any more than we can "sell love" or "negotiate peace."

Worship is a voluntary act of gratitude offered by the saved to the Savior, by the healed to the Healer, and by the delivered to the Deliverer. And if you and I can go days without feeling an urge to say "thank you" to the One who saved, healed, and delivered us, then we'd do well to remember what he did.

—Max

Journal

I worship you, God, because...

For Further Study

To study more about worship read Psalm 86:9–13; 99:5; 100:1–5; Hebrews 10:1–6; 12:28.

Additional Questions

10. Do you feel more worshipful in a group or in solitude?

11. What part does worship play in our path to greatness?

12. In your way of thinking, what is the one bottom line reason why God should be worshiped?

Additional Thoughts

Holiness in a Bathrobe

When your world touches God's world, the result is a holy moment. When God's high hope kisses your earthly hurt, that moment is holy. That moment might happen on a Sunday during Communion or on a Thursday night at the skating rink. It might occur in a cathedral or in a subway, by a burning bush or by a feed trough. When and where don't matter. What matters is that holy moments occur. Daily.

—Max Lucado

1. What do you think makes a moment holy?

____

____

____

____

____

____

A Moment With Max

Max shares these insights with us in his book *Eye of the Storm*.

"All of you who were baptized into Christ have clothed yourselves with Christ."

This morning I "put on" clothing to hide the imperfections I'd rather not display. When you see me, fully clothed, you can't see my moles, scars, or bumps. Those are hidden.

When we choose to be baptized, by lifestyle as much as by symbol, into Christ, the same shielding occurs. Our sins and faults are lost beneath the sheer radiance of his covering. "For you died, and your life is now hidden with Christ in God." Please don't miss the impact of this verse. When God sees us, he also sees Christ. He sees perfection! Not perfection earned by us, mind you, but perfection paid for him.

"For God caused Christ, who himself knew nothing of sin, actually to be sin for our sakes, so that in Christ we might be made good with the goodness of God."

Note the last four words: "the goodness of God." God's goodness is your goodness. You are absolute perfection. Flawless. Without defects or mistakes. Unsullied. Unrivaled. Unmarred. Peerless. Virgin pure. Undeserved yet unreserved perfection.

No wonder heaven applauds when you wake up. A masterpiece has stirred...

So while you groan, eternity gasps with wonder. As you stumble, angels are star struck. What you see in the mirror as morning disaster is, in reality, a morning miracle. Holiness in a bathrobe.

2. What amazes you most about the fact that God sees you through the holiness of Christ?

____

____

____

____

3. What kinds of things make this concept difficult to accept?

____

____

A Message from the Word

[8]In this Scripture he first said, "You do not want sacrifices and offerings. You do not ask for burnt offerings and offerings to take away sins." (These are all sacrifices that the law commands.) [9]Then he said, "Look, I have come to do what you want." God ends the first system of sacrifices so he can set up the new system. [10]And because of this, we are made holy through the sacrifice Christ made in his body once and for all time.

[11]Every day the priests stand and do their religious service, often offering the same sacrifices. Those sacrifices can never take away sins. [12]But after Christ offered one sacrifice for sins, forever, he sat down at the right side of God. [13]And now Christ waits there for his enemies to be put under his power. [14]With one sacrifice he made perfect forever those who are being made holy.

Hebrews 10:8-14

4. How do you think it would have affected you to take one of your farm animals to the temple and watch it be killed for your sins?

5. Why do you think the Bible says that Jesus "sat down" when his work on the cross was over?

6. How would you explain Christ's sacrifice to someone who was unfamiliar with the story of the crucifixion?

More from the Word

[4]Come to the Lord Jesus, the "stone" that lives. The people of the world did
not want this stone, but he was the stone God chose, and he was precious.

[5]You also are like living stones, so let yourselves be used to build a spiritual
temple—to be holy priests who offer spiritual sacrifices to God. He will
accept those sacrifices through Jesus Christ. [6]The Scripture says:

> "I will put a stone in the ground in Jerusalem.
> Everything will be built on this important and precious rock.
> Anyone who trusts in him
> will never be disappointed."

[9]But you are a chosen people, royal priests, a holy nation, a people for
God's own possession. You were chosen to tell about the wonderful acts of
God, who called you out of darkness into his wonderful light. [10]At one time
you were not a people, but now you are God's people. In the past you had
never received mercy, but now you have received God's mercy.

1 Peter 2:4-6, 9-10

7. What does it mean to you that you belong to God?

8. What is the significance of the illustration of Christ as a cornerstone of a building?

9. How does it affect our lives when we live day to day with the knowledge that God sees us exactly as we are?

My Reflections

Go ahead and get dressed. Go ahead and put on the rings, shave the whiskers, comb the hair, and cover the moles. Do it for yourself. Do it for the sake of your image. Do it to keep our job. Do it for the benefit of those who have to sit beside you. But don't do it for God.

He has already seen you as you really are. And in his book, you are perfect.

—Max

Journal

What kinds of things do I needlessly try to hide from God?

For Further Study

To study more about holiness Romans 6:22; 1 Corinthians 1:30; Ephesians 4:20–24; Hebrews 12:10.

Additional Questions

10. Describe the difference between what God sees when he sees us through Christ's righteousness and when he sees us in our own righteousness?

11. How do you see the mercy of God in your own life?

12. What kinds of things do we do to make ourselves look better to God?

Additional Thoughts

CPSIA information can be obtained at www.ICGtesting.com
Printed in the USA
BVOW041557261211

279088BV00002B/74/P

9 780849 954313